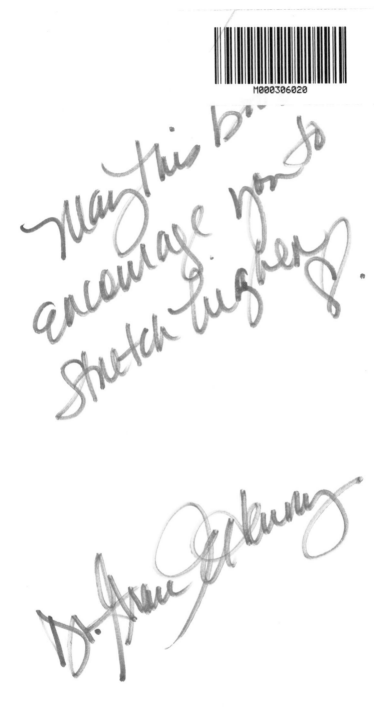

May this b[ook]
encourage you to
Stretch Higher!

Dr. Anne Eskury

Listening to My Mom Will Change Your Life

21 Life Changers for Living Relentlessly

Dr. Grace E. Henry

DEDICATION

To the woman whose love continues to cover me.
Thank you for everything.

ACKNOWLEDGEMENTS

There are so many people who have been a part of this journey. I may not call every name but know that I honor your presence in my life.

To my immediate family ("The Queen Mother", Miriam, Joy, Lefty, Eladia, Milana), you all are an ever-present help. You helped to ensure that even the most obscure Life Changer made it into the book! Your energy around making sure this book was the best representation of our family gave me the strength to move forward.

To Aunt G—you rock! I don't know where you keep the time vault of pictures from the 60s to present, but you are the keeper of the family history. Thank you for chronicling our life journey. I definitely won out in the aunt department.

To my "Dream Team" (Ebony, Joan, Jessica, Joy, Erica)— who would believe we spent so much time trying to convince the author (me) to go with the book cover you liked? You all are amazing women with amazing talents. You gave of your time when I had nothing but free food to give to you. Thank you for sharing your gifts with me. May the return on your investment in me exceed anything you could imagine. I truly could not have accomplished this dream without you.

To the members of Dominion who contributed to this journey—thank you for your invaluable support, your love, and your belief in me.

To my GW family—you listened to me talk about this book for years. You stayed invested in every twist and turn. You counseled me, availed me of your resources, and cheered me on. I am grateful that I spend eight-plus hours per day with such amazingly talented and caring people.

To my friend network in the "DMV", the Virgin Islands and across the globe—Thank you.

Lastly, to The One who knew me even before I was formed in my mother's womb. Thank you for blessing me with the gifts and talents that will bless and change the lives of others. It is an honor to be called to such a great responsibility.

INTRODUCTION

Growing up in the Henry household meant *My Mom* would frequently endeavor to share her wise words with my three siblings (Miriam, Jason, and Joy) and me. Of course, as a teenager, you don't quite understand the value of your parents, and so *My Mom*'s words were often taken for granted. As an adult, however, I have had the opportunity to view, first hand, the impact *My Mom*'s words have had on others. At first, when friends would rant about her advice, I would respond, "My *who* said *what* to you?" To me, she was just *My Mom*...the woman who didn't allow me to hang out with my friends when I wanted to. The lady who made me do chores and yelled at me if I didn't do my homework quickly enough. But you know, *My Mom* used to say "just live a little..." meaning that life will truly teach you the lessons that you won't learn through the words of others. At this point in my life, I have come to know that I do not always have to "live the lesson" to learn the lesson. The purpose of this book is to help direct you in learning lessons without having to live them. **I call these lessons "Life Changers".** Some will make you laugh and some may even make you cry. All will inspire you to think about the small steps you can make in your life that will make a big difference.

This book is also a representation of me doing more than just talking about a goal, but pursuing it. As a kid, my favorite beverage was Coca-Cola and I would find ways to accessorize this beverage of choice. So as a teen I would pour a glass of soda and would 'jazz it up' with lemon or lime. In my college years, I started noticing commercials for Coca-Cola with Lemon and Coca-Cola with Lime. I remember thinking, "Wait a minute! Coca-Cola is making money off something I've been doing for years?" I had the idea of squeezing lemons and limes into my soda, but I did nothing with the idea, and I lived long enough to see someone else put that idea in motion. Now fast forward to about a year ago when I decided on a professional life challenge of saying "yes" to anything I would normally say "no". Well, halfway through my journey, I one day turn on the television only to hear writer/producer Shonda Rhimes talk about her "Year of Yes" –she decided to say "yes" to things she would have said "no". Shonda not only talked about this decision, but she was also pointing us to her book and TEDx talk on this very topic. This was my Coca-Cola moment all over again. Now a little older and a little wiser, I have decided that I won't let this happen again. I have decided that I will no longer sit on an idea, convinced that it isn't "good enough," only to see someone else bring the same exact dream into fruition. *My Mom* has always said that there is nothing new under the sun. Just as a dream has been given to you, if you do not pursue it, someone else will. This book is me doing more than talking about a dream and later seeing it pursued by someone else.

"Why 21 Daily 'Life Changers?" I'm sure most of you have heard the saying, "It takes 21 days to form a new habit." This concept originated in the 1950s when Maxwell Maltz, MD noticed a recovery pattern in his cosmetic surgery patients. No matter the medical procedure, he observed that it took his patients a **minimum** (NOT maximum) of 21 days to become accustomed to their new state. Dr. Maltz applied this concept to create a theory on behavioral change and habit formation, and I am applying this concept to affecting long-term change in your life. The format of this book recognizes that there is nothing necessarily magical in the number "21", rather the magic is in the intention, repetition, commitment and consistency doing something for 21 days will require. By reading this book, you are committing to a change journey where you will no longer settle for what is, but will embrace what can be. You are committing to "living relentlessly". What does that mean? It means you will push forward, no matter what obstacles are standing in your way. No matter the valid reasons for you to quit, you are determined to relentlessly pursue your dreams, your passions and your purpose. This is what I have decided to do. I invite you to take the journey with me.

TABLE OF CONTENTS

DAY ONE

Daily Life Changer #1: Monkeys know which tree to climb.
Keyword: Self-Confidence

I recently had a conversation with a colleague who was frustrated by her supervisor. He would send her emails inquiring about her whereabouts several times during the day. She would receive emails from him over the weekend where he would expect her immediate response. He was unrelenting and she was at her wit's end. What I found so interesting about her situation is that whenever I would interact with him, he would be nothing but nice. This gentleman always noticed when I was wearing a new dress or wore my hair in a different style. Whenever he came across professional articles from which he thought I could benefit, he would email them to me. The same man who made my friend miserable was, by many accounts, a great colleague to me. He knew which tree to climb.

Do you know someone who always picks on those they perceive to be weaker or more sensitive? *(Or are you that person?)* Essentially, as with any "bully"-type situation, certain personalities identify those whom they feel can be easily intimidated or taken down. These personalities never go up against those they perceive to be bigger or stronger— at least not for very long. Rather, these personalities tend to search out those whom they deem to be an easy target. According to *My Mom,* do not be the tree that gets climbed. Individuals who are looking to take advantage of you project their insecurities and insufficiency onto you. They try to knock you off-balance and cause you to second-guess yourself. They leave you feeling like you are the one with the problem and you are the one in need of changing! *My Mom* often says "Grace Henry, let people's issues be THEIR issues". Essentially, know that you are enough just the way you already are. Learn to speak up for yourself and let your self-confidence shine through. Surround yourself with others who can help you develop and become a stronger version of yourself. Do not be the tree that gets climbed. You deserve greater!

"Talk to yourself like you would to someone you love."
(Brene Brown)

Takeaway: Speak up for yourself. Let your self-confidence shine through.

In order to CHANGE your life, ask yourself:
1. In what places of my life do I need mentoring and further development?
2. In what ways can my life be enhanced if I simply learned to believe in myself and my abilities?

DAY TWO
Daily Life Changer #2: Every day is fishing day, but not every day is catching day.
Keyword: Patience

Life is filled with many waiting periods. A pregnant woman goes through nine months of carrying a baby, and several hours of labor to bring that baby into the world. The average employer wants a new employee to have a college degree, which adds an additional four years of schooling after all the years invested to navigate through elementary, middle and high school. When starting a new job, a new employee usually must wait approximately 90 days before they can access their benefits. I could go on… If you focused on the amount of time in life that you spend waiting, you could get discouraged. However, the joy of hearing a baby's first cry; the excitement of degree conferral; the ability to take a day off from work without concern that your paycheck will be reduced, makes it worth the wait. Goals require a daily commitment. Some of those days, however, are simply not glamorous. In actuality, they can be downright hard.

In 2003, I decided to pursue a terminal degree. I knew that pursuing a doctorate was an intense journey so I wrote out a timeline and approximated that I would complete the degree in four years. That didn't seem too long considering that it would take less time than it took me to complete my bachelor's and master's degrees combined (six years)—or so I thought. A four-year doctoral journey was my plan and I intended on sticking to it. Well, life had other plans. What was supposed to be a four-year journey turned into a nine-year wait that included working a full-time job, becoming the caregiver for both *My Mom* and brother Jason; and assisting my younger sister, Joy, with the raising of her

3

daughter, Milana. Oh, did I mention that during that time period I dealt with a fire, two moves, the passing of my brother, and the loss of two dissertation chairs which translated into a two-year void of having no one to sign off on documents that would allow me to complete my degree? Needless to say, I probably would have popped anyone in the face who would have tried to encourage me during this period with the Life Changer "Every day is fishing day but not every day is catching day" because everything around me made me feel like there was no longer a need to attempt to fish. I wish that I could tell you that I continued to feel motivated and I endured life's challenges with style and grace (pun intended). I didn't. In 2011, I made the decision to drop out of my doctoral program because I felt it had become too hard. I convinced myself that life was sending me every signal that achieving this goal was "just not meant to be" and so I created a plan to break this news to *My Mom*. I could get into the specifics but I will spare you the long details. What I will share is that when I was at my lowest, I crossed paths with a woman named Susan. My encounter with her changed my educational trajectory. In the two years prior to our meeting, I had made absolutely no progress. Within ten months of meeting her, I not only made progress, but I actually caught fish! Dr. Susan Swayze came into my life and through her commitment as a fellow educator, she reminded me that Every day is fishing day. Every. Single. Day. Because of her support and my commitment to my dream, I successfully defended my dissertation on March 7, 2012, and finally obtained the degree that I started way back in August 2003—nine NOT four years later.

According to *My Mom*, you will not always feel like a champion. However, your feelings cannot be the driver of your dreams. Were it up to your feelings you would probably be one of the most unpredictable persons anyone could ever meet. Feelings are so fragile and so variable. They are valid but not reliable. Making progress in your life requires a daily commitment. Every day is a day to build your dreams and to work toward your goals. Every day may not be a day to catch, but that should not stop you from fishing.

"Patience is not simply the ability to wait – it's how we behave while we're waiting." (Joyce Meyer)

4

Daily Life Changer #2: Every day is fishing day, but not every day is catching day.

Takeaway: You will not always feel like a champion, so do not let your feelings be the driver of your dreams.

In order to CHANGE your life, ask yourself:
1. Has life's waiting periods distracted me from a daily focus on developing my talents?
2. In what ways can my life be enhanced if I truly committed to the work that is required to accomplish my dreams?

DAY THREE
Daily Life Changer #3: Walk 'bout fool is better than siddown (sit down) fool.
Keywords: Laziness; Fear of failure

My sister, Joy, moved to Maryland from the Virgin Islands with the intentions of pursuing a career in journalism. One day, we went shoe shopping and I distinctly remember Joy picking out a pair of nude flats and telling me she was buying them as a "down payment" on the journalism-related position she intended to get. A few months later, while wearing those nude flats, my sister got offered a production assistant job at a local TV station. We were both elated! Joy explained to me that it was an entry-level position that would eventually propel her into a more stable and fulfilling role.

My sister worked that job for over five years and a role that was supposed to be a temporary stepping-stone started to appear rather permanent and unfulfilling. Joy would be out of the house by 3am, get back home around 1pm to take a quick nap, and would then get up and be back out of the house to go to class throughout the late evening. The last two years of Joy's employment in this position was fraught with her complaining about the dead-end nature of the job, stagnant wages, and no opportunities for advancement. I listened and listened but I eventually got to a point where every time she started to complain I would ask her, "Ok Joy, what you are going to do about it?" I'm sure this frustrated her at times but my pushback was to get her to see that she could either allow life to act on her, or she could act on life.

One day after I had a strenuous day at work, Joy said to me, "Grace, I've decided to quit my job." I perked up immediately, because I was expecting to hear more complaints about her job.

We had countless conversations about that job, but *this* conversation was different from all others. There was thoughtfulness in her reasons and decisiveness in her tone. Her resolve reminded me of something I learned when I was pursuing a master's degree in counseling. We were taught about "locus of control"—the degree to which you believe you have some control over the outcomes of life. Individuals who have an internal locus of control believe that they can exert some influence on how things turn out for themselves. Whereas individuals with an external locus of control believe that environmental forces act upon them and that "fate" controls what happens. For the five years that my sister worked in this position, I would offer that her locus of control was more externally situated. She worked hard waiting (and hoping) that those in positions of power would notice her and reward her accordingly. When she realized this was not happening, she decided to take control of her personal destiny. My sister decided that if the choices were to stay in a dead-end job that had gone nowhere in five years (siddown fool), or to launch out into unknown waters (walk 'bout fool)—she would choose the latter.

According to *My Mom*, nothing new will be accomplished if you sit idly by and allow life to just happen. Stepping out of the 'familiar zone' is scary but you will never know what could be if you refuse to get up and do something. For some, it's a sign of laziness. For others, it's a sign of fear. Either way, remember, "walk 'bout fool is (ALWAYS) better than siddown fool."

> *"Laziness is a secret ingredient that goes into failure. But it's only kept secret from the one who fails."*
> *(Robert Half)*

> *"You gain strength, courage, and confidence by every experience in which you really stop to look fear in the face. You must do the thing which you think you cannot do."*
> *(Eleanor Roosevelt)*

Takeaway: It is better to make a foolish mistake than to never bother trying.

In order to CHANGE your life, ask yourself:
1. Do I become so overwhelmed with the thought of failing that I convince myself that there is no point in trying?
2. In what ways can I enhance my life if I stop overthinking an action or activity, and just do it?

DAY FOUR

Daily Life Changer #4: What don't kill does fatten.
Keyword: Resilience

One thing I can tell you about West Indian folks is that they are obsessed with weight—*your* weight. One minute you've lost too much weight and everyone wants to feed you—"Chile, you looking too small!!" The next minute you gain a mere 1.8 lbs and folks are ready to stage a "fork intervention". Clearly you can't win for losing. Anyway, if you have not already guessed, this Life Changer is the West Indian version of, "What doesn't kill you makes you stronger."

I recall hearing this Life Changer from *My Mom* at times when I could probably just use a hug. *My Mom* was about toughening us up! She was all about developing self-efficacy—the ability to believe that you can control external situations. Let's consider the scenario that I fell and tripped. *My Mom* would, of course, walk up to me to check to see that I was alright. Once she established that the only thing hurt was my pride, *My Mom* would say, "Let me tell you something. What don't kill does fatten, Grace Henry."
Thanks, Ma! Now can you please get me some Neosporin?

To build resiliency, *My Mom* would constantly remind you that since you're not dead—you're fatter. Picture that! Now that I am older, I defer to this Life Changer version on resilience. I am an educator by profession, so it is my natural inclination to look up the meaning of words. After hearing this Life Changer for the 1000th time, the academician in me decided to do some empirical research on the meaning of the word "fatten." When I finally looked up the word, I found a few definitions that spoke to me:

Fatten (verb): 1) to enrich; and 2) to make more substantial.

11

Remember this meaning the next time you try on a new pair of jeans...but I digress!

I have not always connected to the "What doesn't kill you makes you stronger" saying because I am unsure that I have emerged stronger from every situation that caused me physical or emotional harm. When my brother, Jason, passed away in 2007 at the age of 37, it hurt me to my core. That loss was truly unbearable. Friends and family were there to support me which has gotten me to a place today where that grief no longer overtakes me. Even so, my heart and emotions struggle to connect to thinking that the experience of losing my brother made me stronger, and it may just be semantics, but I can definitely see how my character has been enriched. That loss taught me a valuable lesson on the power of vulnerability, as it taught me how to accept the help of others.

According to *My Mom*, "What don't kill does fatten" means that you should endeavor to learn from each experience. Relish the fact that the page has turned and you have come out on the other side of a situation that seemed insurmountable. Even if you came out looking battered, bruised or broken, know that you have been made more substantial. You are more enriched. You are—yes—fatter! You know better, and you will be able to do better. You may not be at the place where you currently believe it, but in time you will look back and see that you have come out victorious.

"My scars remind me that I did indeed survive my deepest wounds. That in itself is an accomplishment. And they bring to mind something else, too. They remind me that the damage life has inflicted on me has, in many places, left me stronger and more resilient. What hurt me in the past has actually made me better equipped to face the present."
(Steve Goodier)

Takeaway: Every experience enriches your perspective.

In order to CHANGE your life, ask yourself:
1. Have I remained open to learning from the lessons of my past and present realities?
2. In what ways can my life be enhanced if I changed my perspective of experiences from one of disappointment to that of enrichment?

DAY FIVE

Daily Life Changer #5: It's better to say, "Here it is," than "Where it is."
Keyword: Preparation

I had the great fortune of attending Howard University in Washington, DC. One of the student organizations that I was most active in was the Howard University Community Choir. I played many roles in the choir—one of which was the guest artist liaison. One year, for our spring concert, we decided to bring in an amazing soloist who came from a family of amazing gospel singers. I'll refer to her as KCS. Well, it was my responsibility to take KCS where she needed to go while she was in town. During the few days together, I developed a bond with KCS—and she with me—as we went to several shops, restaurants and even local sights. On her final day in Washington, DC, as I was taking her to the airport for her return home, KCS was feeling a bit sentimental about our time together. She said, "Grace, I really enjoyed hanging out with you. I would love to stay in contact. Do you write music?" In that moment, everything within me wanted to say yes. She is an amazing artist and to have her hear my work and potentially be interested in singing my song would have been a dream come true. For as long as I can remember, I have enjoyed singing. *My Mom* can share stories of my "Whitney Houston" and "Celine Dion" years of singing all over the house and in the car. I naturally hear parts and I am known for making up silly songs on the spot to punctuate any discussion. So what was the problem, you may ask? Well, despite having been a singer for most of my life I never carved out time to put pen to paper. I considered saying yes and then rushing to write a song to send to her. However, because I had never, at that point, written a real song, I knew that I would not have a song that I would want her to hear anytime soon. In that moment, I regretted my lack of preparation and had to answer her honestly—"No, KCS, I don't write music".

To this day, every time I see her on television or hear one of her songs, I think, "What if I had a written a song and was able to produce it when she asked that question?" How different would my life potentially be if, in that moment, I was actually able to say: "Here it is!" instead of, "Where it is"? According to *My Mom*, you must always be prepared or as she likes to say, "Don't get ready. Be ready." There is nothing like having to pass up an opportunity of a lifetime because you did not get that certification, or practice for that interview, or go back to school to finish your degree. We have all heard the adage—"Success is preparation meeting opportunity". *My Mom* reminds us that sometimes opportunity only knocks once and when it knocks you want to be able to say, "HERE IT IS!" So ask yourself, when opportunity pops up at your door, will you be prepared?

> *"There is no secret to success. It is the result of preparation, hard work, and learning from failure."*
> *(Colin Powell)*

Takeaway: Success comes when preparation meets opportunity.

In order to CHANGE your life, ask yourself:
1. In what places of my life am I simply unprepared for the next level of promotion?
2. In what ways can my life be enhanced if I challenged myself to invest time into my purpose and dreams?

DAY SIX

Daily Life Changer #6: Stand up there and call it—see if it comes.

Keyword: Effort

Let me set the scene. As I mentioned earlier, my sister Joy, *My Mom*, and my youngest niece Milana, all live with me. With a household of three generations of women, there is no lack of stories to tell...Anyway, on with this story...when my sister Joy is "looking" for something, it can come off as if she is really just asking my mother to look for it for her (she would probably disagree, though)! This is the way it normally goes—Joy is going back and forth in the house, with much energy, looking for said thing. She doesn't want to ask for help but whatever Joy is looking for is something she typically needs right away. By the time Joy asks for help, she feels like she has sufficiently exhausted all options of where said item could possibly be. She goes, "Mommy, did you see my (let's say) keys??? I had it right here. I didn't move it. I've been looking for my keys all over the house and I just can't find it. I gotta go somewhere and I don't have my keys." Hearing Joy's panic, *My Mom* will assist in finding the elusive thing. What is always so amazing is that *My Mom* will get up and in less than 60 seconds she is almost always able to find the thing that my sister could not locate for hours.

This song and dance routine has gone on for several years, so as you can imagine, *My Mom* has become hip to the game. Lately, when Joy asks for help looking for a lost item, instead of jumping up to look for the missing item, *My Mom* gives a 'dry reply'. She rolls her eyes, sucks her teeth and in her strongest Antiguan accent will say to my sister, "Joy! How 'bout you stand up there and call it and see if it comes". To this, Joy normally huffs in frustration and frets under her breath a "never mind" or "whatever Mommy" response. Clearly, *My Mom* doesn't believe that Joy can actually call the item and it appear. To the untrained ear, one would think that *My Mom* was mocking Joy. Rather, when *My Mom* says, "Stand up there. Call it. See if it comes", she is communicating that you are not truly putting in as much effort to find the thing you state to be so desperate to find.

According to *My Mom,* we cannot wish a thing into existence. Sometimes the acquisition of a thing requires us to do more than we are currently doing. We can fool ourselves into believing we are doing our best, but when our results do not change, we must question whether we are telling ourselves the full truth. We all know someone with great potential that can never seem to move from potential to actualization. These individuals can talk forever about what they plan to do. Because of their energy and passion, we initially believe every word that they say. However, as days turn into weeks, weeks turn into months and months into years, we start to realize that there has been no change in their reality. These individuals are often referred to as dreamers because in most cases, though they seem to be trying, they appear to live in the clouds. What most people need to get to their goals is a vision. Do you have a vision? Or do you just have a dream? The difference between a dream and a vision is a plan. This plan does not need to outline every next step before you. It must recognize, however, that additional, intentional steps must be taken. When it comes to your purpose, without a vision you might as well just "stand up and call it—and see if it comes."

> *"Effort without talent is a depressing situation, but talent without effort is a tragedy."*
> *(Mike Ditka)*

> *"Dreamers dream; achievers achieve. Some will always dream and some will always achieve."*
> *(Ernest Agyemang Yeboah)*

Takeaway: Nothing happens just because we want it to.

In order to CHANGE your life, ask yourself:
1. In what places of my life am I simply "going through the motions" of life without any real drive or ambition?
2. In what ways can my life be enhanced if I devised a plan and created a timeline for completion of at least one goal within the next 6-12 months?

DAY SEVEN
Daily Life Changer #7: Sit on crooked stick till it come straight.
Keyword: Sacrifice

I was fortunate to live on-campus during my undergraduate and graduate years of college. Upon graduation, I moved off-campus and found an apartment. I remember classmates moving into the city into beautiful high-rise apartments and buying beautiful cars. However, my financial reality did not allow for me to live anywhere near the city I had been living in for the last six years of college life. So I moved about 40 minutes away to an apartment that was tiny, in an area that was close to being described as sketchy, and that had a bus stop out front—which was particularly important because at that time I could not afford a car. I scraped up enough money to pay for the first and last months' rent and the security deposit. Once I paid all the related moving expenses (rental truck, electricity, heat, etc…) all I could afford to purchase was a bed and a 27" TV. I had absolutely no furniture so when I went to watch television I would sit on the living room floor to watch. I did not have much, but I remember feeling so happy because this was my first place.

My job situation was not that much different. When I graduated from my master's program, I was 23 years old with very little work experience and found myself working in a temporary wage position. This translated into being paid hourly with no benefits. I had no annual or sick leave. No way to save for retirement and was an at-will employee. This means that at any time they could have told me they no longer needed me and I would have been out of a job with no financial net to catch me.

About three months after getting my job, I caught the flu—for the first time in my life. How lucky was that? I would, however, continue to get up every single day to take a 30-minute bus ride *(I caught this bus for about 3 years!)*, to a 25-minute train ride, with a 5-minute walk to my building, only to walk upstairs to sit in my office with the door closed (to not infect the office) because I needed to work every hour I could to pay my rent and utilities. I had flu symptoms for an entire week and though my body was frail, because of my personal financial responsibilities, I did not stop for one minute. I had to go to work. I continued as a temporary wage employee for nine more months until the paperwork was put in to make the position full-time. Since then, I have moved up in both position and salary, and I still catch the train—but this time it's by choice!

That time in my life was my "crooked stick". I had a master's degree but that didn't ensure that I would start at the top. Because I work in higher education, I hear so many students bemoaning humble beginnings. Somewhere they were convinced that they would have access to their dreams jobs and dream homes upon graduation. I learned during the days of the "crooked stick" that although I had the credentials, I still had to pay my dues. I think the thing that is often missed is that "paying dues" is not an exercise in futility. It is the crucible in which character, perseverance, and resilience are cultivated. My first apartment was not what I had envisioned, but because my rent was so low, as my salary increased, I was able to stick to a rather rigorous savings plan. When I finally decided to move, I had enough of a down payment to purchase my first home—a condominium that was almost three times the size of this apartment.

My Mom says never despise small beginnings. Make the most of your current season in life. Work that first job with integrity and with the resolve that you are gaining the experience and connections you will need for the dream job you are working toward. Go ahead and get an affordable apartment that you share with one or two roommates, instead of spending 75% of your salary on rent. My first apartment was not the most glamorous; my commute to work was not the shortest, and the bus I took to and from work was not the most reliable. Yet, I was convinced that I was living a temporary reality. I refused to be distracted by the life

I saw others living and focused on my own. That decision has made all the difference in the life I live today.

> *"Great achievement is usually born of great sacrifice and is never the result of selfishness."*
> *(Napoleon Hill)*

Takeaway: Do not despise small beginnings.

In order to CHANGE your life, ask yourself:
1. Am I jeopardizing my future because I won't make the sacrifices that are required of me today?
2. In what ways can my life be enhanced if I decided to live/plan my life based on where I will be as opposed to where I am right now?

DAY EIGHT

*Daily Life Changer #8: **You can't plant corn and reap potatoes.***
Keyword: Expectations

Well, well, well...this seems like a Captain Obvious Life Changer. I mean really, who could possibly expect to plant corn and reap potatoes? Despite living in a world of "alternative facts", may I dare say that this would be completely impossible? Yet, in our lives many of us plant one thing—that is to say, devote our time and investment into one thing—and expect to reap something else.

I remember this commercial in the early 2000s. A guy walks up to a scale, stands on it and makes note of his weight. He then gets on a treadmill and runs at high intensity for a few seconds. He gets off the treadmill, runs around the machine and then gets back on the scale to see if he lost any weight. No matter how many times I would see this commercial, I would crack up laughing! This dude actually thought that his high-intensity 30-second workout would change his reality. The purpose of the commercial was to show that resolving to lose weight alone is not sufficient to lose weight. Buying the new workout outfit and going once or twice with your friends is not sufficient. You actually have to put in the time, effort and commitment to get the results you want. Life teaches us that you have to do the behavior that corresponds to the desired result. One would think that was common knowledge, right? I wish that I could say that the mere fact of me writing on this topic would indicate that I have this principle fully in hand, but looking over my life, I can identify many times where my expectations were not equivalent to my actions.

For most of my adult life, I took a big "L" in my dating game. I could always describe what I wanted in a partner: a wonderful

25

guy who has great drive and ambition. A guy who is fully secure in the emotional, spiritual and financial areas of his life. This man is good looking, compassionate and loves to travel! As a rather accomplished, reasonably attractive woman, I would often be asked, "So what's the holdup?" Though I could probably rattle off a valid list of external, societal reasons why I was not married with kids or in a serious relationship, when I decided to get honest with myself, I was finally able to identify an internal, behavioral barrier that contributed to my enduring "Ms. Single" reality.

As you know, I work in higher education and I love what I do. I give my all to students and I work hard to support their needs each and every day. By the time I leave work, do you know what is at the top of my to-do list? Go home, take off my work clothes, jump in my bed, turn off the lights and watch reality television until I fall asleep (don't judge me!). As I reflect on my life through the lens of this Life Changer, I must admit that despite the very real dating obstacles that existed for me as a professional woman, in the area of dating, I planted corn for several years, looking for a harvest of potatoes.

According to *My Mom,* everything in life functions by the same principle. You want friends, yet you are not friendly. You want to make more money, but are reluctant to put in the time necessary to develop your knowledge base. You want a stronger, more intimate relationship with your partner yet you won't explore going to counseling or other ways to renew the spark. Harvest after harvest you keep yielding corn and you wonder what you need to do differently. Well, the solution is well stated in this Life Changer. The only way you will ever reap potatoes is if you start sowing potatoes...

"If we don't plant the right things, we will reap the wrong things. It goes without saying."
(Maya Angelou)

26

Takeaway: You must do the work to get the desired result.

In order to CHANGE your life, ask yourself:

1. Are there areas in my life where my expectations for return are inconsistent with my level of effort?
2. In what ways can my life be enhanced if I increased my effort exponentially?

DAY NINE
Daily Life Changer #9: Too much of one thing (is) good for nothing.
Keyword: Overindulgence

I am sure that you have heard about the health benefits of water. We have been told that if you drink enough water every day, it can help you to feel fuller longer which may lead to weight loss. Water can also help to clear up acne and other skin problems leaving us with a youthful glow. Water also helps to flush out many of the body's toxins and helps us to eliminate waste from our bodies more regularly. Hearing all of this, who wouldn't want to drink water? Our bodies are comprised of approximately 65% water so it would not be hard to conclude that water does the body good. But did you know you can drink too much water? The condition "hyponatremia" is caused when the kidneys become overwhelmed by the amount of liquid it has to process. Though rare, hyponatremia often occurs when individuals, mostly during exercise, drink water beyond thirst. To avoid dehydration, some athletes overcompensate by drinking gallons of water thinking that they are being preventative, not realizing that they are putting themselves in danger. By ingesting too much water, these athletes have turned the "good thing" that is water into something that is good for nothing. In fact, in this case, water has become detrimental.

I suspect if you took a minute to do some introspection, you might find a parallel in your life. What is the 'thing' in your life that started off as a hobby, or a benefit, but now compromises the quality or integrity of your life? I challenge you to do a thorough examination of your life. What do you honestly need to stop doing?

29

According to *My Mom*, there is a tipping point where even a good thing ends up being good for nothing. This goes for everything—including the socially acceptable forms of dysfunction. What are some of those you may ask? Well from experience, I can give you two: the tendency to overwork, and the tendency to be excessively perfectionistic. These socially acceptable forms of dysfunction are rewarded and celebrated, and we are often anointed with the monikers of "hard worker", "high achiever" or simply "boss" as a result. I get it. We all want to be loved and admired but at what cost? Pushing yourself to the point of exhaustion, being proud that you only sleep four hours a night, or regularly painting a "S" on your chest may be good for social media optics, but in the end when our relationships suffer and our health fails we will see that all that public posturing was truly good for nothing.

> *"The mother of excess is not joy but joylessness."*
> *(Friedrich Nietzsche)*

Takeaway: Everything in moderation.

In order to CHANGE your life, ask yourself:
1. Do I have a hard time saying "no" and setting boundaries in my life?
2. How would my life be enhanced if I prioritized balance in all areas of my life?

DAY TEN

Daily Life Changer #10: You can't be too careful but you can be too careless.
Keyword: Carelessness

This is a Life Changer that I would hear *My Mom* recount repeatedly. Things in life happen but *My Mom* has always been the one to point out that you, too, play a part. I remember one day losing my wrist wallet while on my way to work. I normally carry an oversized bag that includes a purse, a change of shoes, lunch, work ID, and a few other random items. So as I was rushing from the subway I started to phish around for my work ID as I ran to the front door of my office building. I located my ID and was able to tap into the building. When I got to my desk, I put down my stuff and opened my purse to retrieve my wrist wallet, but it was not there. My first thought was that maybe I put it in the oversized bag after using it to get off the subway. Nope, it was not there either. My next thought was that in my haste to pull out my work ID, I did not realize I dropped my wrist wallet which contained my debit card, two credit cards, my driver's license and my metro card. I made every effort to remain calm, but at this point I was panicked, to say the least. I spent about 15 minutes retracing my steps in an attempt to find my wrist wallet. I was unsuccessful and so I was left with no other choice but to call the bank to cancel all my credit and debit cards. Approximately two hours later *My Mom*, who by the way lives with me, called me at work and the conversation went a little like this:

Me: Hello?
My Mom: Helloooooo Doc. Are you missing something?

31

Me: Did someone find my wallet?

My Mom: Yes. Someone from your bank found it and they were able to look up your information and found your home number and called the house.

Me: Whew! I am SO relieved

My Mom: Grace Henry! You must not be so careless

Me: It dropped out when I was rushing and phishing in my bag for my work ID

My Mom: Well, why were you rushing?

Me: You know what? I can't even tell you why. I just was.

My Mom: Well, someone found it…this time.

We all know that things like this happen, however, in this situation, *My Mom* felt that in all my haste, I had lost my focus. While I may misplace an item from time to time, because *My Mom* drilled this Life Changer into me, I make it a habit to consciously stop and take note of why I am making any given decision. In this example of losing my wallet, when I was forced to consider why I was in fact rushing, I had no answer. The truth is I was rushing simply out of habit. Rushing around has become something that I've adopted as part of my daily routine.

According to *My Mom*, had I just taken one second to stop, I would have saved myself the heartache of not knowing where my wallet was for two hours. By being distracted, I became careless and never considered that I was possibly putting myself into a vulnerable situation. Sounds familiar? I wonder what this looks like in your life. Where are you so busy *being* busy that you have lost focus? *My Mom* often says, "Do not be so hasty" as a way of encouraging me to take careful consideration of my life. My question to you is: "Have you allowed yourself to be so busy with life's pursuits that you are distracted from the things that really matter?"

> *"Life without caution is like a car without brakes."*
> *(Bamigboye Olurotimi)*

Takeaway: Take careful consideration of the choices in your life.

In order to CHANGE your life, ask yourself:
1. In what places of my life am I simply "too careless"?
2. In what ways can my life be enhanced if I took a moment to refocus and make sure that I am headed in the right direction?

DAY ELEVEN

Daily Life Changer #11: Mouth does lie but belly does true.
Keyword: Truth

This Life Changer makes me think of someone I knew as a teenager. We all started to notice that she was gaining weight. She was never extremely thin so at first it just seemed like a few added pounds. After a while, though, these few added pounds were packing on around her stomach and folks started to ask her directly, "Are you pregnant"? She denied it and said that she had not been eating healthy foods so she was just gaining weight. Even when she started to look undeniably pregnant, she continued to tell everyone she was overeating. This is a sterling example of "mouth does lie but belly does true". Though she lied with her mouth, her figure confirmed the truth.

Another example of this comes from of my guilty pleasures— those paternity test shows. I know, I know, it's horrible, but for some reason, if I am flipping the channels and I come across one of these shows, I must play it out until the end. If you've watched one you know the formula of absolute, resolute insistence of paternity followed by DNA confirmation that the guy is "NOT the father". These shows sometimes throw in a twist where there is a pre-administered lie detector test. The results of the first 1-2 questions usually confirm that they are telling the truth. These potential fathers are seen bouncing around screaming, "I told you! I told you!" ...Oh but this is a television show so of course the producers leave the confirmed lies for the end. What is always so amazing is that this test, which was in the potential fathers' eyes 100% accurate on the previous questions, instantaneously becomes unreliable. These guys thought they were smooth enough to "fool" the test but the awesomeness of the body is that there is always biofeedback. So although your mouth says one thing, the lie detectors track the subtle changes in your body. When you tell a lie, though undetectable to you, your body betrays you with an elevated heart rate and blood pressure, and you begin to perspire. These machines don't care about what comes out of your mouth. Rather it cares what your body confirms.

According to *My Mom*, what is done in the dark comes out in the light. We've all met the person who seems to believe their own lies. They create their own realities. Life has a way, though, of balancing all things out. An important faith leader in my life often says, "There's no such thing as a public you and a private you. There's just one you." Do your words match up with your actions? Can you be counted on to consistently walk in truth? The choice is yours. You can choose to live a life of integrity or a life of deception.

> *"Honesty is the first chapter in the book of wisdom."*
> *(Thomas Jefferson)*

Takeaway: You can fool some of the people, some of the time but you can never fool all of the people all of the time.

In order to CHANGE your life, ask yourself:
1. Are there areas in my life where I am being dishonest in word, thought or deed?
2. In what ways can my life be enhanced if I started to live the truth?

DAY TWELVE

Daily Life Changer #12: Friend in court (is) better than money in pocket.
Keyword: Relationships

I was born and raised in St. Thomas, VI. This 32 square miles of beautiful sun, sand and ocean breezes is something I grew up with and took for granted. Because we are an American territory, we are natural born citizens. Our money is the US dollar, but the currency which trumps the dollar is relationships. I remember growing up and having *My Mom* tell me, "If you ever get stuck needing anything, tell them you're James Henry's daughter." At first, I thought, "No one cares about that," but then there were times that I went to a store and was short on cash and said, "I'm James Henry's daughter," and had the cashier say, "Oh ok. Go ahead. Tell your father he owes me two dollars." My father built a reputation with many people in St. Thomas and the strength of his name got me through sticky situations. I've walked through my life, as a result, with a great respect for a strong name and value for friendships and relationships.

A few years ago, I was feeling stuck in my job situation. I started sending out resumes to jobs that I felt qualified for but I hardly received any responses. These were "cold" jobs where I had no connection but hoped that my resume would open the door for me—it didn't. Then one day, I received an email from an old friend telling me about a job for which she thought I would be a great match. When she told me about it, I admittedly wasn't too interested, but it reported to a friend of hers so I decided to give it a try. This time I got the interview and it was because of my friend. I got the job because my qualifications took me over the finish line. Before hiring me, my (now) boss decided to reach out to

37

people that were not on my list of references. She went as far back in my past as she could to find people who worked with me to see what they would say. She could not find one inconsistency because I have held on to this Life Changer for most of my life. Every person she talked to confirmed the identity I have spent the last 18 years developing.

According to *My Mom*, relationships reign supreme. I learned quickly that my bank account may never open doors for me, but the strength of my relationships will. In my pursuit of developing my professional brand, I have been careful to not burn bridges. In those rare instances that I have accidentally lit a match…sorry, let me be honest, in those instances when I was younger and carried "relationship matches" in my back pocket, I have gone back to figure out how to repair that bridge. It takes humility to go back to a friend or coworker and admit, "I was wrong. Can you please forgive me?" We live in a time where people find value in "sticking it" to someone but what is the added value there? When you know better you do better and I've resolved to do better.

My Mom taught me that you can amass all the wealth in the world but if your name is associated with pettiness, untrustworthiness, lack of dependability, lack of loyalty, etcetera, then you have nothing. If people are unable to say great things about you, then your worth is small—no matter what your bank account says.

> *"A good reputation is more valuable than money."*
> *(Publilius Syrus)*

Takeaway: Good relationships are worth its weight in gold.

In order to CHANGE your life, ask yourself:
1. Am I willing to compromise my relationships and reputation for the sake of obtaining a particular status or level of recognition?
2. In what ways can my life be enhanced if I reprioritized relationships over ambition?

DAY THIRTEEN
Daily Life Changer #13: A promise is a comfort to a fool.
Keyword: Gullible

When I was pulling this book together, *My Mom* did not recall ever saying this Life Changer. However, this was a staple in the Henry household. At risk of her disowning me, I will say that I became most acquainted with this Life Changer during some of *My Mom's* bleakest emotional times. For years, I only processed the meaning through the lens of her hurt. You see *My Mom* only seemed to repeat this Life Changer when it came to things my father said. I would say, "Dede (affectionate term for my father) said he is going to do X thing". Of course, I would be so full of hope and expectation because my father said he was going to do something and by virtue of it coming out of his mouth, I knew it was the truth. The only thing that could knock me off my high horse of anticipation was this Life Changer by *My Mom*. As a child, it felt like she waited for me to climb on my excitement perch only to take her "sling and stone" collection of words and BAM! Like that I was brought back to reality. "A promise is a comfort to a fool, Grace Henry" is what she often said. I must say, I am not sure what felt more devastating—the fact that she would say that, or the fact that she was sometimes right.

As an adult, I process this Life Changer very differently. Although I became acquainted with it through *My Mom's* hurt, I now see it as a perspective shifter. I make a concerted effort to ensure that every promise I make is accompanied by confirmatory action. There was a time in the 1990s where to affirm something you promised, your statement would be followed by a "Word is Bond!" acclamation that your word is enough proof that said thing will happen. This Life Changer has forced me to shift perspectives within my intimate relationships. As a young girl, I believed in the fairy tale romance and I was hooked on the concept of "happily ever after". I still do believe that happy is out there but now I make sure that corresponding actions accompany the promises of "happily ever after". Have you ever been in a relationship where the person whom you love keeps selling you on dreams that for some reason never seem to materialize? Their promises are so well meaning and because you believe in their dreams you stay. I think commitment is important, so staying makes sense. However, in some relationships, disappointment after disappointment occurs, yet you wait because you want to believe them. Hell, they want to believe themselves!

According to *My Mom*, absent of action, a promise is an empty shell. What good is a promise that stands alone? If I promise you a ride but I leave you waiting at the side of the road, what good is my promise in ensuring that you get home? If I promise you that I will change, but you see the same me day in and day out, how comforted have I left you? At some point, the rubber must meet the road. As the saying goes, "Don't just talk about it. Be about it".

> *"I called his broken promises heartbreaking, and he called it growing up."*
> *(Jarod Kintz)*

Takeaway: Absent of action, a promise is an empty shell.

In order to CHANGE your life, ask yourself:
1. Am I ignoring signs in my life that clearly indicate that I am foolishly holding on to a promise?
2. In what ways can my life be enhanced if I lived in reality instead of the land of wishful thinking?

DAY FOURTEEN

Daily Life Changer #14: All the King's horses and all the King's men couldn't put Humpty Dumpty back together again.
Keyword: Letting Go

My Mom has said many things to me; however, this Life Changer is in the top three most memorable Life Changers I have ever heard *My Mom* share. Most of you reading this book grew up hearing the story of Humpty Dumpty. I was first introduced to Mr. Dumpty in elementary school and it just seemed like a fun nursery rhyme. I must admit that I was that kid who initially heard it and thought, "An egg is not alive, so this story is fake!" Yes, yes, even at a young age, I overanalyzed the world! Even as I went along with the story, my young mind wondered, "Why would an egg sit on a wall?" I can't say that I've ever recalled the story of Humpty Dumpty again, until the day I talked with *My Mom*.

Let me paint the scene. I was upset. I was involved in what I believed to be a misunderstanding and I was distraught that the explanation of my motives to this individual was not enough. It seemed that no matter what I said or did, the individual with whom I was having conflict held steadily to their interpretation of my motives and intentions. One thing I know about myself is that I really dislike being misunderstood. I am devastated when my actions are experienced opposite of my intention. I am confident that most people who know me would describe me as loyal, dependable and *real*. I rarely communicate what I don't mean. I value friendships and I value the wellbeing of others. My feelings are sincerely hurt when I find myself in a situation where I feel that others don't experience this side of me. I normally don't seek advice from my West Indian mother because it usually starts off with a long story and I can be a bit impatient waiting for her to get

41

to the point! This day, however, I knew I needed her counsel and was willing to be patient enough to hear her stories because I couldn't find an answer to remedy this problem.

I had gone into the Dr. Grace E. Henry emotional toolbox and had come out empty handed. I did not know how to solve this issue and worse yet, I couldn't get to an emotional place of being ok with the way things were. I decided to go into *My Mom's* room with tears streaming down my face, heart heavy with hurt and mind truly at a loss of what to do next. *My Mom* has lived with me for over ten years and she immediately knows when I am overwhelmed and in serious need of her advice. Though many times when I've sought her advice she immediately launches into the "telling Grace what to do" portion, this day she patiently listened to my story and after she told me to stop crying, she wisely and softly uttered this refrain: "All the King's horses and all the King's men couldn't put Humpty Dumpty back together again." Normally, I wouldn't get it. In this moment, however, it was as if I heard this refrain for the first time. I realized that what was frustrating me most in the situation was that I kept trying and trying to get this person to see me the way I see myself, but they either could not or would not see past their version of reality.

According to *My Mom*, some things simply cannot be changed. Some things just are. For most of us, that is a hard reality to accept. Mr. Dumpty's demise represents a reality broken beyond repair. Despite everyone in the kingdom coming together to utilize their collective human resources, Mr. Dumpty could not be put together again. That day I learned from *My Mom*, that no matter how hard you try or how much you wish, there are certain realities wherein once things change, they may never again be the same.

> *"Some people believe holding on and hanging in there are signs of great strength. However, there are times when it takes much more strength to know when to let go and then do it."*
> *(Ann Lander)*

Daily Life Changer #14: All the King's horses and all the King's men couldn't put Humpty Dumpty back together again

Takeaway: Some situations may always remain the same.

In order to CHANGE your life, ask yourself:
1. Am I holding too tightly to a reality that has expired?
2. In what ways can my life be enhanced if I learned to look forward instead of looking back?

DAY FIFTEEN
Daily Life Changer #15: Every grin ain't a smile.
Keyword: Authenticity

I was born and raised in St. Thomas, VI. I would describe Virgin Islands' culture as very direct, or as anthropologist Dr. Edward T. Hall would say, one that is high-context. High-context cultures are collectivistic and relational. In other words, a high-context culture is a community of people where there is a high value on trust and honesty. In such a culture, a simple "I got you, man" is enough to finalize an agreement because one's word is one's bond. Growing up, I was surrounded by a culture where what you saw was what you got. If someone was mad at you—you knew it. If they didn't like you—you knew that too. If they disagreed—they said it. If they were bothered—they would show it. This was (and continues to be) my preferred way to communicate.

In 1993, I moved to Washington, DC to attend college. This was the first time in my life that I encountered a low-context environment. It took me awhile to realize that not everyone was comfortable as I was in sharing exactly what was on their mind. I also came to realize that someone who seemed friendly was not always a friend. I did not learn these things without first getting my feelings hurt, unintentionally offending others, and sometimes questioning whose friendship I could count on.

I remember a professor for my doctoral program telling me to guard what information I shared on my dissertation progress. This was confusing because I found my classmates to be rather friendly and helpful. This professor said, "I can see the confused look on your face and maybe you won't have to encounter what I did when I was doing my degree. I had to learn the hard way that not everyone is happy for you." Luckily, I never had the experience that he had while completing my degree, but I have since experienced what he was talking about. I've had people close to me copy my ideas, try to block my progress, and try to sully my reputation. I've also had people in my life who were happy for me as long as they felt like their lives were still "on top". When opportunities arose that gave me more visibility or accolades, their "happiness" appeared to be tested. *My Mom* would suggest that some people attach themselves to you because of how they think they can leverage your friendship. Others will be more selfish in their friendship and in these relationships, you will find yourself giving more than receiving. My experiences and the experiences of close friends have shown me that the people we most expect to be there for us, especially when times get hard, are sometimes the ones nowhere to be found. So be careful.

Now, this Life Changer is not about mistrust. It is about guarding the gift that is friendship. Most friendships consist of love, trust, dedication, and loyalty. Your friendship should be given to those who will treasure it and understand its value. According to *My Mom*, just because someone befriends you, smiles with you, or shares your space, does not mean that you will develop a relationship that will last or be beneficial to you. *My Mom* would encourage a healthy dose of skepticism as you open yourself to new experiences. Just keep in mind that just because someone is grinning, does not mean they are smiling.

> *"The word "friend" is a label anyone can try on. You decide who is best suited to wear it."*
> *(Carlos Wallace)*

Takeaway: Surround yourself with those who are genuine and true.

In order to CHANGE your life, ask yourself:
1. Do I need to take inventory of the individuals who I allow the ability to influence my life?
2. In what ways can my life be enhanced if I learned to identify the patterns connected to the relationships that currently exist in my life?

DAY SIXTEEN

Daily Life Changer #16: There's something in the mortar beside the pestle.
Keyword: Honesty

I had absolutely NO idea what this Life Changer meant for years. I had never heard of a mortar and pestle, and I barely remembered seeing one. A mortar and pestle is a useful device consisting of a stick like object used to crush the contents within a bowl. The mortar and pestle are often used to crush herbs into a paste or powder, and in the preparation of medicines. When this Life Changer was used in my home, it was to signify suspicion that there was more to a given story. I would hear *My Mom* say this when I was a young kid eavesdropping on her adult conversations. I would see *My Mom* talking on the phone and it was only a matter of time until I would hear her say, "Mmhmm… well you know there is something in the mortar beside the pestle". Because I was a kid I normally never found out what that was, but I was filled with glee just thinking about the mystery of what she could be talking about.

As an adult, this Life Changer has hauntingly followed me on the job and in my personal life. I work in the collegiate environment with high student interaction. Students are notorious for coming in with stories about why something did or did not occur. These stories are sophisticated and refined, but just like how your mom could always sniff out your lie, so can I. At the end of a student explanation, I normally respond with, "Now are you ready to tell me the rest of the story?" My ability to uncover the truth has also been useful in relationships. Youthful relationships can be filled with strong memories, torrid passion, and many "untruths". It is easy to be "so in love" that one avoids acknowledging when a story does not add up. It sometimes feels better to just let "sleeping dogs lie" but according to *My Mom*, getting to the root of a situation is a requisite to understanding how to find a resolution. Whether it is your lie or the lie you accept, authentic living requires submersion in honesty.

If you want to live in freedom you must know the truth. You must live in the truth. You must embrace the truth—no matter how ugly. Nothing else in life can give you the freedom that brings peace to your inner spirit. You can try to fool others and even yourself by being selective with what you choose to share, but true wholeness is only achieved when one reveals what is in the mortar besides the pestle.

> *"Honesty is the first chapter in the book of wisdom."*
> *(Thomas Jefferson)*

Takeaway: Full honesty is needed for true growth.

In order to CHANGE your life, ask yourself:
1. Do I seek out the truth of a situation or am I comforted by believing a lie?
2. In what ways can my life be enhanced if I committed to being honest in all my ways and accepting that, only, from others?

DAY SEVENTEEN
Daily Life Changer #17: The same day the dog dead, ain't the same day it stinks.
Keyword: Aftermath

Let me start by saying that I lived in a household of over five dogs and several cats. My favorite dog growing up was "Velveteen". We had her for several years and when she died, I was never again able to allow myself to connect to another animal. She meant that much to me. I have since become allergic to dogs and so it has helped me to keep Velveteen as the standard bearer of dogs in my mind's eye. So I hope that helps you understand that this Life Changer is not a callous dismissal of the loss of a beloved pet.

Now, let's get to the heart of this Life Changer. One day, as I was putting lotion on my legs, I noticed a long scratch. I mean this scratch was at least 5-6inches long. I showed a friend of mine the scratch and she asked if it hurt. I said, "Actually, I don't even remember rubbing up against anything over the last few days. I'm not even sure when I did this." Because it was now a scab, I figured that this encounter happened several days prior. It clearly didn't hurt in the moment, but it was significant enough to leave a trace many days later.

Growing up, this Life Changer served as a constant reminder that not all of life's outcomes are experienced immediately. I remember running in the house and into one of the doorposts. *My Mom* said to me, "Grace come let me rub that with some medicine." I told her that it wasn't necessary because "it's not hurting me". She then did her West Indian "You clearly don't know, chile" laugh and responded, "The same day the dog dead ain't the same day it stinks, Grace Henry". Whether it was a slip on a wet floor or a stumble down the stairs, *My Mom* would relentlessly remind us with this Life Changer to pay immediate attention to the situation even if we felt nothing was wrong. Though *My Mom* usually used this Life Changer to refer to health issues, life has shown that it is applicable to other parts of life.

Have you ever been put on the spot to make an immediate decision? Think about how telemarketers call on the phone—many times calling you by your first name as if you all are best friends—with amazing travel packages, throwing several deals which end with "Once this conversation is over the terms of the deal expire." Anxiety producing isn't it? Should you take the deal? Is it a deal at all? Can you find better? Well, what do you normally do? Is your decision driven by the imagery of you walking on a sandy beach with clear blue water sipping a Mai Tai in the middle of winter? Or maybe, you are like me and you are quickly running the numbers in your head trying to calculate everything. Whether you accept the deal right away or let the deal disappear, could there be a long-term impact to saying "yes" or "no"? Well, the world might not end when you hastily decide to take the travel deal, but what about when you hastily decide to quit your job because you've had it with your supervisor? What happens when you decide to take your married co-worker up on a dinner invitation? What are the long-term implications of your decision to walk away from a relationship during a rather rough patch? Will life be different if you decide to turn down a four-year college scholarship to take what appears to be a well-paying job right out of high school? I do not know these answers. I can't even pretend to know. While every decision does not require weeks, months, and years of meditation, I am suggesting that you should always count the cost.

According to *My Mom*, you must always anticipate future outcomes. Just because you do not currently see signs of impending change, does not mean it is not coming. Things are not always as they seem.

"Don't make permanent decisions based on temporary feelings." (Paul Tsika)

Takeaway: The total effect of an action may not show itself immediately.

In order to CHANGE your life, ask yourself:
1. Do I have situations in my life that have the potential to positively or negatively impact my life?
2. In what ways can my life be enhanced if I pause to consider the ramifications of my actions or inactions?

DAY EIGHTEEN

Daily Life Changer #18: When your neighbor's house catch fire, wet yours.
Keyword: Compassion

There are some people in life that seem to delight in the downfall of others. This is something that I've never truly understood. Even when things happened to folks who were either "former friends" or the group I call, "never friends", I could always sympathize if they lost a job or a loved one. However, there are some people that will simply take advantage of any moment to "hate" on someone else. They always seem to be up-to-date on someone's impending divorce, failed business or repossessed car. Sometimes they are overt about spreading gossip, but of late, I've noticed that social media has converted how this message is conveyed. No longer do you get the in your face, "Girllllllllllll let me tell you what happened to so-and-so." Nope! Now the gossip is enjoyed through the guise of soliciting prayers and positive energy. You've seen the social media caption which reads, "I think we need to keep Sara in our prayers because her partner cheated on her, emptied all of their bank accounts, and now she's about to lose her house. #StandingWithYouGirl #WeGotYourBack #ThoughtsandPrayers." Ok, this might be a bit of an exaggeration but I think you get my point. Though the modus operandi may have transformed, the buried motivation for this type of gossip remains the same. These individuals buy into the belief that we are all fighting for the same "piece of the pie". Your setback, your disappointment or your incomplete goal, in their minds, gives them a leg up to get ahead of you!

Well, according to *My Mom*, today might be my day to deal with adversity, but tomorrow may be yours. Your struggle may not look like someone else's addiction or broken relationship, but don't think for one moment that this means that you are somehow exempt from the trials of life. Sometimes the things we go through are a direct result of our poor decisions. Other times, life simply has decided to deal us a "bad hand" through no fault of our own. While it might be human nature to wonder what a person did to "deserve" what they are going through, I challenge you to dig deep and find a heart of compassion. The next time a friend, co-worker, family member or even a "frenemy" is going through a hard time, try giving them an encouraging word or sending up the prayer you talked about. If you deposit good deeds into the bank of others, when life eventually requires a personal withdrawal, there will be goodwill from which to pull. Through it all, remember to "rejoice with those who rejoice and weep with those that weep", or as *My Mom* would put it, "When your neighbor's house catch fire, wet yours."

> *"Don't rejoice when your enemies fall; don't be happy when they stumble."*
> *(Proverbs 24:17 NLT)*

Takeaway: Preparing for the trials of life is best done by supporting others in need.

In order to CHANGE your life, ask yourself:
1. Do I find myself secretly finding pleasure in the misfortunes of others because deep down inside, I am unhappy with where I am (or who I am) in life?
2. How would my life be enhanced if I learned to put the needs of others before the insecurity of myself?

DAY NINETEEN

Daily Life Changer #19: Howdy and thank you, breaks no bone.
Keyword: Respect

As basic as this Life Changer may sound, it can be a rather challenging thing to practice. We all have that one person who knows how to get under our skin. You know, that person who when you're walking down the hallway and you see them before they see you, you start ducking, dodging, or straight up ninja rolling under the desk right next to you? Ok, that might be a bit dramatic and you probably have never "stopped, dropped and rolled," but I'm sure you have pretended to be reading a very important text or email when they stop by your office unannounced. We either find this person to be annoying or worse yet, we simply do not view them to be worthy of our time or attention. Still doesn't sound like you? Ok well, let's try this…what about the facilities employee who comes and empties the office trash daily? Do you know his or her name? Could you pick them out of a lineup, or are these living breathing individuals with families (and first and last names) invisible to you? We live in a society where we are obsessed with ourselves and our importance. Our schedules are packed and we have so much to accomplish in a day. We don't mean to walk into the office without speaking—we just have a deadline to make. We are busy being busy and we do not realize that this fundamental principle can get us further in life.

I recently sang at my friend's sister's funeral. It was a packed service but there was someone who stood out from the crowd. This gentleman cleans one of the floors in my office building. He walked up to me and told me that he was my friend's cousin. He introduced me to another family member as "one of the nice people I work with." I had the distinct thought that this would have been an awkward interaction if I ignored his existence at work just because he was "the cleaning guy". I can think of countless times where those who are sometimes rendered invisible have helped me simply because I choose to see them every day. Of late, I've also decided to "see" others, that in the past I've chosen not to see. Though I can find legitimacy in ignoring the loud, bossy, or uncool coworker, I've decided that it takes more strength of character to choose to see them, as well. We've all heard that we should treat others the way we would want to be treated, but do we? According to *My Mom*, there is always room to be pleasant to others. Acknowledge others—even when you have valid reasons to not like them. The way others treat you should not change the way you treat them. It doesn't hurt to be nice. Your back won't get stiff, your head won't start throbbing, and not one of your bones will be broken, just because you extended the olive branch of politeness. I promise you, you'll be ok...remember that the next time "you know who" comes walking down the hall.

> *"Rudeness is a weak imitation of strength."*
> *(Eric Hoffer)*

Takeaway: It does not take much effort to be kind and respectful.

In order to CHANGE your life, ask yourself:
1. Have I become self-absorbed with my own life that I do not notice what's going on in the lives of others?
2. In what ways can my life be enhanced if I took a moment to identify and address the areas in my life where I have become jaded and unkind?

DAY TWENTY
Daily Life Changer #20: Bucket go to well every day; one day the rope gon' buss.
Keyword: Character

I am always amazed when I hear of bank robbers that rob multiple banks. I mean really? When was the last time you heard of a bank robber getting away with robbing a bank? Maybe if these criminals had a "one and done" mentality, then they might be more successful, but for some reason, once is never enough. Isn't that just like life? It's almost an innate greed that rises up within us and says, "That was easy. Let's do it again."

This leads me to recall the late '90s movie "Set It Off" (one of my favorite movies), which was about an ensemble cast of women who wanted to get ahead in life. So, as with any good crime action movie, these women decide that the best way for them to get ahead in life, was to...you guessed it, rob a bank! I can't remember the exact scene when it was decided, but I do remember that they were all nervous and argued back and forth about whether it was something they should try. Eventually, each of their life circumstances became so dire that what was once something that seemed far-fetched appeared to be the only answer to their issues. Wow! I could stop right there and talk at length about what happens when desperation drives your decisions. It's like going grocery shopping hungry. You end up with a cart full of items that you never considered buying in the first place... Anyway, these women robbed their first bank and got away with it! There was a scene with them rolling around in the money and throwing the money up in the air. They thought they had made it. For that moment, they enjoyed the high of getting away with robbing a bank and receiving a big payout. Some of the women thought, "We have enough money to get us out of the hole—let's never do this again." However, they ended up losing the money and were left with no other option but to rob more banks.

As with so many other decisions in life, what started off as a free choice turned into a dreadful requirement. So this cast of women robbed banks again and again. Each time, these women got bolder and bolder; and more confident. With this confidence, however, came carelessness. They got sloppy. These women no longer focused on covering up their tracks because they had fooled the authorities before, and their experience convinced them that they could do it again. This sense of invincibility inevitably became their downfall. They eventually got caught, and all but one of these women lost their lives. What started off as fun and games eventually required of them the ultimate price.

Now I am aware that the average person is not about to rob a bank, but if we are truly honest with ourselves, we could identify dysfunctional behaviors that we participate in just because we can and we have. This may be as harmless as regularly taking supplies from the office or fudging your vacation leave numbers. Maybe you're that person who regularly manufactures work gossip or orchestrates discord so that you can always come out on top. Ouch, the truth hurts, doesn't it? Still doesn't sound like you? Well, maybe you are attracted to taking even more exhilarating risks so you take a tax deduction for which you don't qualify. For those of you who are more private, this may look like a decision to engage in risky sexual choices, extramarital affairs, or the use of prescription or recreational drugs every so often.

Whatever your "bucket" may be, according to *My Mom*, if you continue to take risk after risk, one day your time will come. Trust me it will. Some people call it arrogance, others call it stupidity, but whatever it is that makes you believe you are untouchable is simply misleading you. There is a price to be paid for every decision that is made in life. Sometimes the price is exactly what we hoped. Other times, the price is for far more than we bargained.

"There is a price to pay for doing wrong and there is a reward for doing right." (Recovering Grace Blog)

Takeaway: Choose to do the right thing even when no one is looking.

In order to CHANGE your life, ask yourself:
1. Am I currently engaging in activities that could one day be destructive to my personal or professional life?
2. In what ways could my life be enhanced if I endeavored to live a life that radiates with integrity?

DAY TWENTY-ONE

Daily Life Changer #21: God made bread before He made mouth.

Keyword: Provision

I'll be honest and say that I struggled with whether or not to include this Life Changer. As I thought about writing this book, I was intent on not including an "overtly" faith-related Life Changer. However, no matter how hard I tried, I just could not end this book without including a Life Changer that truly embodies the person that is *My Mom*. Ask anyone who knows *My Mom* and the universal descriptor would be a "woman of faith." To know Mrs. Gwendolyn Michael Henry is to know a woman who submits everything to prayer. Through prayer, *My Mom* raised four kids without health insurance. Through prayer, *My Mom* sent four kids to college though she earned less than $20,000/year. Through prayer, *My Mom* endured the loss of her only son. Through prayer, *My Mom* has survived over a decade after being given six months to live. So although you may or may not submit to the belief of a higher calling, *My Mom* does. As such, it is befitting that I share this final Life Changer with you. According to Merriam-Webster, worry is defined as:

To think about problems or fears; to feel or show fear and concern because you think that something bad has happened or could happen.

Even the most confident people in the world can share something they constantly worry about. My worry is normally around having enough. I would characterize my childhood experience as one where we had just enough to get by. I remember having a "school shoe" and a "church shoe". Whenever I would get home from school or church, I would be told to immediately put up my shoes to extend its life. I also recall asking permission to get anything out of the refrigerator. This, too, was done to preserve what little we had. Though we never went without and I am decades away from that reality, there is a part of me that continues to be impacted by growing up with just enough. Despite my degrees and my professional success, there is a part of me that is committed to the "side hustle" (e.g. teaching classes, writing books, and conducting seminars and training sessions) because I am afraid of losing the ability to financially support my life and the lives that depend on me. It is sobering to admit that within Dr. Grace E. Henry, lives the little girl who still remembers watching *My Mom* pray to God that she'd have enough money before going on grocery shopping trips.

This Life Changer "God made bread before He made mouth," is truly one that can change your life if you ingest its full meaning. According to *My Mom*, even before you were thought of, provision for your needs was made. Do you *believe* this? *Can* you believe this? This Life Changer requires both vulnerability and dependence—the "kryptonite" of the independent man or woman. Society encourages us to be strong and handle everything on our own while looking great all at the same time. I remember in the late 1980s a deodorant company admonished us to "never let them see you sweat"! The reality is many of us are trying to fix all our problems without relying on anyone. The one thing I've started to do, particularly when I get overwhelmed by bills and life's realities, is stop and count my blessings.

A few years ago, I purchased a home to accommodate the family members who live with me. There are times where I find myself overwhelmed at the thought of paying the mortgage. In these times, I pause to give thanks that this little island girl *has* a mortgage. Two years ago, my big feet decided to shrink in size (who knew that could happen?). Since then finding shoes is almost impossible. When I find myself complaining about having so many shoes that now do not quite fit, I pause and give thanks that this island girl owns more than one "school shoe" and one "church shoe". When I find myself renting a room in the hotel of worry and despair, the reality that pulls me out every time is the knowledge that as I look back over my life, I see that everything I needed was provided. When I look even closer, I can see that most of those provisions were made even before I recognized my need. Now I didn't always tangibly have things, but I had access and favor. People helped me and offered my name when opportunities arose. Friends and strangers helped pull me along the way. *These* are your provisions. They've already been made—you just have to access them. So, the next time you are overwhelmed by worry or overcome by fear, remember these words from *My Mom*, a woman of faith, "God made bread before He made mouth."

> *"Worry never robs tomorrow of its sorrow, it only saps today of its joy."*
> *(Leo F. Buscaglia)*

Takeaway: You already have everything you need to succeed in life.

In order to CHANGE your life, ask yourself:
1. Have I surrendered the direction of my life over to the authority of worry?
2. How would my life be enhanced if I trusted that there is a divine master plan already laid out for every step that I will ever take?

BONUS DAY

BONUS Daily Life Changer #22:   Even a good excuse is still an excuse.

Keyword: Tenacity

This book is about listening to *My Mom* but I couldn't leave out this BONUS Life Changer from *My Dad* (who I call "Dede") which has shaped so much of me. This is the only Life Changer that I recall ever hearing Dede say to me throughout my childhood. Those closest to me would probably describe me as extremely driven and accomplished, however, the childhood version of me would be described as anything but driven. I was a shy, quiet child who often shut down when confronted with obstacles. My feelings were easily hurt and opposition easily discouraged me. I cannot remember the first time Dede said this to me, but I do recall a specific instance of telling him that I couldn't get a school project done and giving him a list of barriers that I was encountering. I was frustrated because I needed to complete my assignment, but there were legitimate issues that were preventing me from getting it done—or so I thought. After Dede listened to my entire story, he didn't say much. He simply said, "'Papa' (his late father) used to tell me as a young boy that even a good excuse is still an excuse". That's all he said to me after I gave him my long struggle story. Though his words were few, they smacked me dead in the face. I had just spilled my guts to him about all the things standing in my way of accomplishing my goal, and instead of supporting me, I felt shot down. In that moment, I thought to myself, "'Papa' was unsympathetic to you, and now you are being the same way to me." I felt like Dede's response was tremendously heartless considering the legitimate interference I was experiencing in my life. As I said, this is the only thing I remember ever hearing *My*

65

Dad say and it became a refrain that I heard more often than I hoped.

This Life Changer was rehearsed so much to me that at some point I started to preemptively ask myself, "Grace, are you making excuses?" waaaaaaaay before bringing a concern to *My Dad*. I think it's fair to say that this Life Changer became a part of my inner voice. Even when I moved away to attend college, in the face of any obstacle, I felt like I could almost hear *My Dad*'s voice in the back of my head saying, "Grace, even a GOOD excuse is still an excuse". Because of this, I found the strength to overcome most hindrances that I encountered instead of letting them overcome me.

According to *My Dad*, life will try to knock you down with everything it has, but your will to succeed must be stronger than the most valid of obstacles. That's hard to hear, isn't it? We want to be validated. We want others to sympathize with us. Depending on the situation, it can feel like it's just easier to believe that things "were just not meant to be", rather than to push that mountain out of the way. As I reflect, I've learned that what *My Dad* was trying to teach me with his Life Changer was that in the end, none of that matters. He wanted to build a resolve in me that couldn't be shaken. I now describe myself as a problem solver and a resilient life champion. I credit this Life Changer with changing the way I interact with the world and how I navigate through life. Today, I extend that lesson to you.

Although someone may have hurt you, betrayed you, deceived you, taken from you, or even lied to you; do not let your "valid reason" keep you from completing what you have set out to accomplish. Your dream must be worth more to you than the validity of the struggles against you. Whatever you want in your life will not be given to you. You must fight to get it! So fight!

> *"He that is good for making excuses is seldom good for anything else."*
> *(Benjamin Franklin)*

Takeaway: Don't let life's obstacles throw you off course.

In order to CHANGE your life, ask yourself:
1. Am I using life's realities as a "good excuse" to not pursue

my purpose?

2. In what ways can I start, TODAY, to move past every obstacle, and reach toward my visions and dreams?

Daily Life Changer Questions Review

1. In what places of my life do I need mentoring and further development?

2. In what ways can my life be enhanced if I simply learned to believe in myself and my abilities?

3. Has life's waiting periods distracted me from a daily focus on developing my talents?

4. In what ways can my life be enhanced if I truly committed to the work that is required to accomplish my dreams?

5. Do I become so overwhelmed with the thought of failing that I convince myself that there is no point in trying?

6. In what ways can I enhance my life if I stop overthinking an action or activity, and just do it?

7. Have I remained open to learning from the lessons of my past and present realities?

8. In what ways can my life be enhanced if I changed my perspective of experiences from one of disappointment to that of enrichment?

9. In what places of my life am I simply unprepared for the next level of promotion?

10. In what ways can my life be enhanced if I challenged myself to invest time into my purpose and dreams?

11. In what places of my life am I simply "going through the motions" of life without any real drive or ambition?

12. In what ways can my life be enhanced if I devised a plan and created a timeline for completion of at least one goal within the next 6-12 months?

13. Am I jeopardizing my future because I won't make the sacrifices that are required of me today?

14. In what ways can my life be enhanced if I decided to live/plan my life based on where I will be as opposed to where I am right now?

15. Are there areas in my life where my expectations for return are inconsistent with my level of effort?

16. In what ways can my life be enhanced if I increased my effort exponentially?

17. Do I have a hard time saying "no" and setting boundaries in my life?

18. How would my life be enhanced if I prioritized balance in all areas of my life?

19. In what places of my life am I simply "too careless"?

20. In what ways can my life be enhanced if I took a moment to refocus and make sure that I am headed in the right direction?

21. Are there areas in my life where I am being dishonest in word, thought or deed?

22. In what ways can my life be enhanced if I started to live the truth?

23. Am I willing to compromise my relationships and reputation for the sake of obtaining a particular status or level of recognition?

24. In what ways can my life be enhanced if I prioritized relationships over ambition?

25. Am I ignoring signs in my life that clearly indicate that I am foolishly holding on to a promise?

26. In what ways can my life be enhanced if I lived in reality instead of the land of wishful thinking?

27. Am I holding too tightly to a reality that has expired?

28. In what ways can my life be enhanced if I learned to look forward instead of looking back?

29. Do I need to take inventory of the individuals who I allow the ability to influence my life?

30. In what ways can my life be enhanced if I learned to identify the patterns connected to the relationships that currently exist in my life?

31. Do I seek out the truth of a situation or am I comforted by believing a lie?

32. In what ways can my life be enhanced if I committed to being honest in all my ways and accepting that, only, from others?

33. Do I have situations in my life that have the potential to positively or negatively impact my life?

34. In what ways can my life be enhanced if I pause to consider the ramifications of my actions or inactions?

35. Do I find myself secretly finding pleasure in the misfortunes of others because deep down inside, I am unhappy with where I am (or who I am) in life?

36. How would my life be enhanced if I learned to put the needs of others before the insecurity of myself?

37. Have I become self-absorbed with my own life that I do not notice what's going on in the lives of others?

38. In what ways can my life be enhanced if I took a moment to identify and address the areas in my life where I have become jaded and unkind?

39. Am I currently engaging in activities that could one day be destructive to my personal or professional life?

40. In what ways could my life be enhanced if I endeavored to live a life that radiates with integrity?

41. Have I surrendered the direction of my life over to the authority of worry?

42. How would my life be enhanced if I trusted that there is a divine master plan already laid out for every step that I will ever take?

43. Am I using life's realities as a "good excuse" to not pursue my purpose?

44. In what ways can I start, TODAY, to move past every obstacle, and reach toward my visions and dreams?

Author's Biography

Grace E. Henry, Ed. D. is a dynamic speaker, writer, author, and educational strategist. She has spent the last twenty years working in the areas of leadership, diversity, and college student engagement. With a background in psychology and education, Dr. Henry is uniquely qualified to help people find their life's purpose and pursue their destiny. She has trained students, administrators, and thought-leaders in the public, private, and religious sectors on developing leadership skills, self-awareness, and relentless determination. Dr. Henry attended Howard University where she received a bachelor's degree in psychology and a master's degree in counseling psychology. She completed her doctor of education degree in Higher Education Administration from The George Washington University. Dr. Henry is a native of St. Thomas, VI and now resides in Maryland where her *Mom* lives with her. Dr. Henry is available for keynotes, workshops, seminars, and educational and diversity consulting. She may be contacted at drgracehenry@gmail.com.

52743082R00049

Made in the USA
San Bernardino, CA
29 August 2017